A BOSTON TRADER

Macdonald

Contents

Introduction

This book tells the story of two children, John and Patience, who lived in Massachusetts, in north-eastern America, in about 1730. Many of the people who lived in America at this time were farmers, like the children's parents. They cleared the forests to plough fields, raise animals and grow crops like maize and beans. Their lives were often hard; there was no money to spare for luxuries, and each member of the family had to work hard to make sure that they grew enough food to last them through the bitter winters. They lived in houses built largely out of wood cut from the forests all around them. Their furniture was simple, and built to stand up to hard wear rather than for comfort.

In this story, John and Patience go to visit their wealthy uncle, who is a merchant in the busy port of Boston. He has made a lot of money from shipping timber, fish and whale-oil to Europe and the West Indies and bringing back European goods to America, where they fetch high prices. The children are amazed to see the fine brick house where their uncle lives, and to compare the luxurious way in which he lives with their simple life back on the farm. They also meet their cousin Priscilla, with whom, they find, they have very little in common!

Some of the furniture and luxuries found in Boston homes at this time are illustrated at the end of this book. In addition there are suggestions for books to read and places to visit.

A Surprise Invitation

'Mother! Mother – there's a letter for us from Boston!' yelled John. He rushed into the family parlour. His heavy boots spread farmyard mud all over the scrubbed wooden floor. Mother sighed. More housework! She stretched out her hand to take the letter.

'Bring it over here, John,' she said. 'And next time, leave your boots at the door!'

Mother looked at the letter and recognised her brother Samuel's handwriting. She opened the letter with trembling hands. 'I wonder what's the matter!' she said anxiously.

Letters were a rare event for John's family; so rare, that they usually meant bad news. John, his parents, his brother Richard and his sister Patience lived in the little village of Saxmundham, Massachusetts, which lay three miles from the main road that linked the big towns of Boston and New York. If there were any letters for the villagers, the post rider left them at the general store at Blithborough, the nearest town on the main road. The letters waited there for days at a time until the grocer's boy from Blithborough brought them over with his weekly delivery of stores to the Saxmundham shop. Uncle Samuel had written his letter over ten days ago.

Mother finished reading it and smiled with relief. 'It's all right,' she said. 'I was so worried, but it's good news, after all! Your uncle has written to invite you and Patience to go and visit him in Boston. You'll have to leave the day after tomorrow. You can travel with Richard. He'll keep the pair of you in order!'

Richard was nearly grown up. He was leaving home to go to Boston to work with Uncle Samuel, who was a wealthy merchant and trader and owned several ships. He had offered to train Richard so that he could take over the business from him when he retired.

Mother's voice was brisk. 'Now John, Patience! We must get things ready for your journey!'

7

On the Road

Uncle Samuel's letter had said that he would meet Richard, Patience and John at Blithborough.

'I'll wait there in my new carriage,' he had written. 'I have business to do with some of the tradesmen. Afterwards, we can travel back to Boston in comfort!'

Mother had been very impressed when she learned about Uncle Samuel's new carriage. She told Father, as soon as he came in from milking the cows.

'Hmph!' said Father. 'He's getting mighty fine, is your brother Samuel. New carriage and a big house! I'm surprised that he still wants to know his poor country relations. We're just farmers, not rich like all his friends in Boston!'

Mother looked shocked. 'Jacob Thoroughgood, I'm ashamed to listen to you! My brother Samuel is a righteous, God-fearing man, who's not too proud to help his needy relations. He's giving Richard a great opportunity to make his way in the world, taking him on as his assistant, and don't you forget it! Mind you,' she added, 'I can't say that I think very much of that

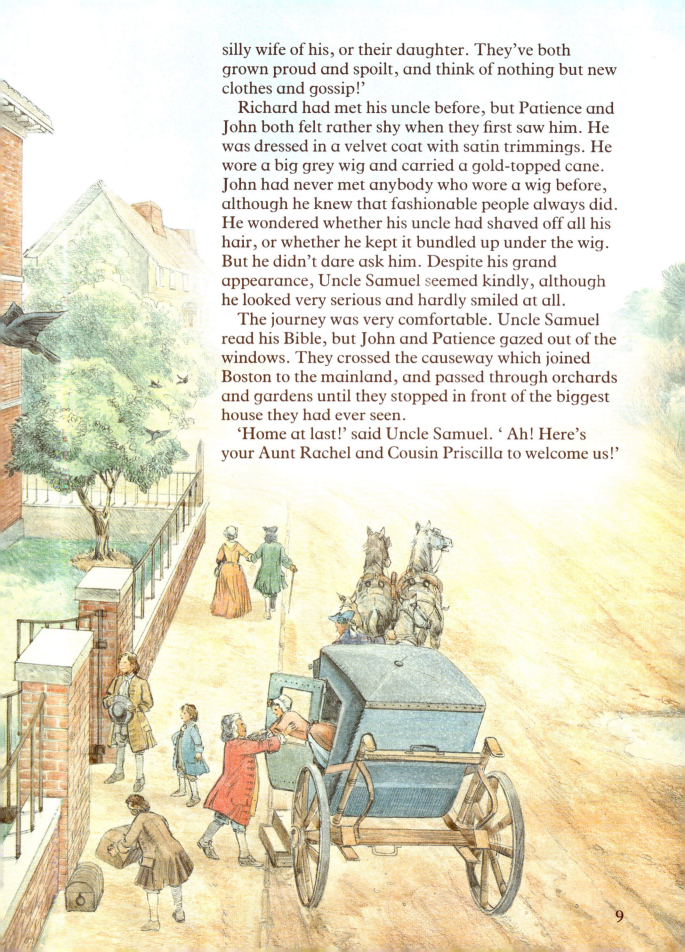

silly wife of his, or their daughter. They've both grown proud and spoilt, and think of nothing but new clothes and gossip!'

Richard had met his uncle before, but Patience and John both felt rather shy when they first saw him. He was dressed in a velvet coat with satin trimmings. He wore a big grey wig and carried a gold-topped cane. John had never met anybody who wore a wig before, although he knew that fashionable people always did. He wondered whether his uncle had shaved off all his hair, or whether he kept it bundled up under the wig. But he didn't dare ask him. Despite his grand appearance, Uncle Samuel seemed kindly, although he looked very serious and hardly smiled at all.

The journey was very comfortable. Uncle Samuel read his Bible, but John and Patience gazed out of the windows. They crossed the causeway which joined Boston to the mainland, and passed through orchards and gardens until they stopped in front of the biggest house they had ever seen.

'Home at last!' said Uncle Samuel. ' Ah! Here's your Aunt Rachel and Cousin Priscilla to welcome us!'

At the Wharf

That night, the children slept in beds with hanging canopies, in bedrooms with carpets on the floor. The beds had feather mattresses, which were deliciously soft, not like the lumpy ones at home stuffed with corn husks. They were not used to such luxury.

'John! Patience! Richard!' called Aunt Rachel's maid. 'Come downstairs! Breakfast is ready!'

Aunt Rachel and Priscilla were already sitting at table in the breakfast parlour.

'Just think!' whispered Patience. 'A special room just to have breakfast in!'

'Now, children,' said Aunt Rachel. 'This morning, Richard and John will go with Uncle Samuel. Patience, you will come with Priscilla and me. Priscilla will lend you one of her cloaks, then no one will see that frock of yours.'

'That is very kind, Aunt,' replied Patience. She knew she ought to be polite, but inside she felt furious.

Uncle Samuel led the boys through the crowded streets. 'These new brick buildings – were all put up after the great fire,' he said. 'In the past, most houses in Boston were made of wood, but that's forbidden now. It catches fire too easily. And over there,' – he pointed to a very grand building – 'is the new Town House where the Government sits. We merchants meet there too, to fix up business deals. Now, let's walk down here and we'll come to the Long Wharf.'

John and Richard looked at the ships moored at the Long Wharf with interest. There must have been twenty or thirty of them, gently swaying with the tide. A fresh, salty smell of the sea drifted towards them.

'Ah, here's my office!' said Uncle Samuel. He shouted for his clerk. 'Mr Henry! How are we getting on with loading the *William and Susanna*?'

'She's nearly ready to set sail for Bristol,' replied the clerk. He glanced down at the pages of his ledger. 'Let me see, yes, we've loaded 18 tons of wood, 507 barrels of tar, 7 barrels of whale oil and 40 barrels of cranberries. That's it, I think!'

'Fine!' said Uncle Samuel. 'Now boys, would you like Mr Henry to show you round her before she sails?'

On Board Ship

The deck was wet and slippery beneath John's feet. He clung on to a huge coil of rope as the ship swayed. Mr Henry and the ship's Master laughed.

'Don't worry, my lad! You'll get used to it!'

John soon recovered his balance. From the deck he could see the whole harbour.

'There must be hundreds of ships anchored here,' he said. 'I didn't know that Boston was so big.'

'You shouldn't really call all of them ships,' said Mr Henry, sternly. 'Only the big ones with three masts, like this one, are ships. There are lots of different types of vessel. For example, that one over there is what we call a ketch, and that one just hoisting her sails is a brigantine.' He peered through his telescope, and then passed it over to John. 'If you look over by the lighthouse,' he said, 'you can just see a schooner.'

'I can see the sailors working on deck!' said John, excitedly. 'And the ship's cat, asleep in the sun!'

'That schooner's come in from a coastal patrol, I expect,' said the Master. 'She's a new sort of vessel, and very fast. We keep the harbour well-defended. That's Fort William over there, where the guns are. And we have a system of warning signals, too. If enemies are sighted then we light a fire on Beacon Hill to warn everybody. But most ships come here peacefully, just to trade. They bring tar and timber from the north, and fish and oil. And we get ships bringing sugar and molasses from the West Indies. Your uncle owns a distillery where they're made into rum, and fine rum it is too!'

They went below decks. John peered into the hold, where the cargo was stored, and into the cramped, stuffy underdeck where the crew slept on hammocks slung from the ceiling. It was very dark down there. He liked the Master's cabin, and Mr Henry's. They were like little rooms, with proper tables and chairs, and huge chests to store all the maps and charts.

'If we have passengers, then they have the cabin next to mine,' said the Master, 'though there's not a lot of room. The voyage to Bristol takes 26 days with a good wind but, more often than not, we're at sea for nearly a month. It's a long way to England!'

The Coffee House

They joined Uncle Samuel on the quayside.

'I usually stop at the coffee house on the way home,' he said. 'It's a good place to discuss business. Most of the merchants call in there and you hear all the latest news. You learn what's going on in the world at the coffee house long before you read it in the newspaper!'

The coffee house was a long plain room with a sanded floor and scrubbed tables. There was a fire burning merrily and the room was filled with pipe smoke and the sound of talk and laughter. A strong smell wafted from a row of pewter pots that were being kept warm in front of the fire. John supposed that it was the smell of coffee, though he had never tasted it.

'Come and sit down here,' said Uncle Samuel to the boys. 'I've ordered coffee for us, and I'll smoke a pipe before we go. Your aunt doesn't like me to smoke at home. She says the smell hangs round too long.'

John took a cautious sip from the cup that the servant brought him. He thought it tasted very odd.

Uncle Samuel was busy talking to Richard. 'Yes, that's how the first Bostonians made their fortunes,' he said. 'They sold timber and fish. They soon realised that they could make more money that way than by growing crops. They sold timber to England, where they're very short of wood, and brought back cloth and furniture and all sorts of fine things that they make over there. Craftsmen's wages are very high in Massachusetts, so it's cheaper to import manufactured goods from England than to make them over here. Surprising, isn't it?'

Richard agreed with his uncle that it was. 'And do you make your money in the same way, and by hiring out ships to other merchants?' he asked.

'Indeed I do!' replied his uncle. 'Now, we must be getting home. Come along, John!'

Back at the house, Patience greeted her brothers enviously. 'You've had a good time,' she said, 'but all I've done is visit a library and walk in the Mall. And Aunt Rachel and Priscilla have done nothing all day but talk about the ball they plan to go to next week. It's been so boring! I'd rather see a ship. I'd rather be at home!'

Bad News

'Uncle Samuel's house is so grand that I daren't touch anything,' sighed John.

'You'd better not!' exclaimed Patience. 'We don't want any breakages!'

The rooms of Uncle Samuel's house were lined with painted panelling, and the floors were covered with Turkish carpets. The furniture had been made by the best craftsmen out of expensive walnut-tree wood.

'Some pieces were made specially for us in England,' said Priscilla, grandly. 'And these blue and white dishes are very precious. They've come all the way from China.'

Patience looked nervously at John, but he showed no sign of wanting to touch them. She was glad that Cousin Priscilla didn't know how simple their home was. Instead of carpets, they had just one painted floor-cloth, made of rough canvas. And their furniture had been made from coarse oak by the local carpenter.

In spite of Uncle Samuel's kindness, John and Patience were glad when Saturday came, and it was time to leave for home. Aunt Rachel and Priscilla were still sitting at the breakfast table when a messenger was shown into the parlour.

'I've come from Mr Henry, sir,' said the messenger. 'He told me to tell you that a schooner has just come into the harbour. She has brought bad news, I'm afraid. Her Master told Mr Henry that he had seen a ship like your *Sophia* being attacked by French pirates off the Azores Islands about a fortnight ago!'

'Let us pray that he is mistaken!' said Uncle Samuel. 'But this is dreadful news! I must get down to the harbour straight away to see what more I can find out.' He turned to Patience and John. 'I'm afraid this means that I won't be able to take you home today, my dears. And tomorrow is Sunday, and it's not right to travel then, so you must stay with us until Monday. You are most welcome, of course!'

'Not Monday!' screeched Priscilla. 'That's the day of the ball! You promised to take us! You know we can't go alone! You can't take them home then!'

'It looks at if we've got a long wait ahead of us,' thought Patience.

The Sermon

'I think that it's ridiculous to make such a fuss about the Lord's Day,' complained Priscilla, on Sunday morning. 'You could have travelled perfectly well today! The Governor's daughters – it's the Governor who is giving the ball, you know – well, the Governor's daughters say that in England people would laugh at our ideas. We're so old-fashioned!'

Patience was shocked. It was bad enough having to stay on in Boston when Priscilla was obviously so anxious to get rid of them. But it was even worse when Priscilla talked in such a way about the Sabbath.

Priscilla laughed at her cousin's horrified face. 'You are a country innocent!' she said. 'But don't worry, I don't want to do anything really sinful, like playing cards, on the Lord's Day! Do you know, they actually shut the town gates and stop the ferry on Sundays, as if Boston were a prison. You're not allowed to walk by the sea or on the common, however hot it is.'

Later that morning, the whole family went to the service at the South Meeting House. It was a plain, square building very like the one the children went to back home, only much bigger. Uncle Samuel's pew was at the front because he was so important.

The Minister preached about what he called the Right Way. 'The Puritan way of life is the only way that pleases God!' he said. 'People who find fault with the Puritan Way are sinners! Their words show that they have not been chosen for Life Everlasting!'

Patience hoped that Priscilla was listening carefully to all this, but she rather doubted it.

In the afternoon, the Minister continued his sermon to the townspeople. 'Your ceaseless gossip, your lavish spending on fine clothes, and worst of all your foolish love of dancing will lead you all to Hell!' he thundered. He got so carried away that he forgot to turn his hourglass over and spoke about the evils of dancing for an hour and three quarters. Uncle Samuel looked very worried. Perhaps he should forbid Priscilla to go to the ball?

Fashionable Boston

On Monday morning, Patience and John felt that
they were getting in everyone's way. Uncle Samuel
and Richard were in a hurry to get down to the docks
straight after breakfast. Even while the family were
still eating, they were busy discussing plans to
safeguard Uncle Samuel's other ships from attacks by
pirates.

Aunt Rachel and Priscilla were in a great state of
panic about the ball that evening. They had so much
to do to get ready! Soon after breakfast they set out
to do some last-minute shopping.

'I must have some new ribbons!' said Priscilla.

'And I need a new fan!' said Aunt Rachel. 'Now
come along, you two!'

John and Patience followed them miserably. But,
once they were outside, they soon felt more cheerful.
There was such a lot to see. Unlike their own village,
where the only shop sold just basic necessities, like
soap and candles and cooking pots, the Boston shops
were crammed with all sorts of fancy items. There

were shops selling imported glass and china, delicate gloves and fans, powerful-smelling herbs and spices, and all sorts of things for life on board ship. There was even a bookshop, which sold not only books and pictures but also the latest fashion from England – specially printed paper which you pasted and then stuck on to your walls. Patience thought that this sounded like a most peculiar thing to do, but she had to admit that some of the patterns were very pretty.

When they got home, Aunt Rachel called for a dish of hot tea.

'I am so fatigued,' she said, 'but perhaps this will restore me!'

Tea was the latest fashionable drink. In the afternoons, Aunt Rachel's fashionable friends would call on her, and they would sit and gossip and drink lots of tea out of delicate china dishes. John tried some but poured it into a vase when no one was looking.

'It tastes even worse than coffee!' he told Patience. 'Give me good fresh milk any day!'

21

Dressing for the Ball

The house was in turmoil. Priscilla's new ball gown had only just been delivered, very late, by the dressmaker. Uncle Samuel's best wig, which had been sent to the wigmaker's to be put in curlers and baked, to make the curls stay in place, had come back scorched; the wigmaker had left it in his oven for too long. Uncle didn't think it looked too bad, but Aunt Rachel and Priscilla declared that he couldn't possibly wear it to the ball.

'You'll make us all look ridiculous!' said Aunt Rachel. 'What shall we do?'

In the end, the footman was sent off with Uncle's workday wig, and was told to stay at the wigmaker's to see that it was properly curled this time.

Patience helped her cousin to step into her stiff hooped petticoat and laced her stays for her. Then she helped her put on her beautiful embroidered ball gown, and pinned the stiffened stomacher panel across her chest. Priscilla admired herself in the looking glass. She certainly looked very grown-up.

'You do look pretty,' said Patience, politely.

'I should hope so!' replied Priscilla. 'This gown cost a fortune! You see how it hangs at the back? That's the latest French fashion. Mother has the fashion news sent over to her from Europe in Father's ships. The Governor's daughters are always very keen to see the French fashion pictures.'

She leapt up and hurried into her mother's bedroom. Soon she was back, carrying a tiny silver box. 'I knew there was something missing!' she said. She opened the silver box, dipped her finger in it and dabbed something on to her face. Then she leaned back to admire her reflection.

Patience was amazed to see that Priscilla had stuck a little round piece of black plaster on her face. 'What's that for? To hide a smallpox scar?' she asked.

Priscilla laughed scornfully. 'No, you fool!' she said. 'It's a face patch. In England all elegant people wear them. The Governor's daughters—'

'Well, I think it looks very silly,' said Patience, and she left the room. She felt that she would scream if she heard another word about the Governor's daughters.

In the Kitchen

Patience and John watched as their uncle, aunt and cousin walked down the wide staircase in all their finery. Aunt Rachel's gown was as costly as Cousin Priscilla's. Uncle Samuel wore a very fine embroidered waistcoat. His workday wig had been nicely curled and powdered, and he looked very handsome. 'Even so,' Patience thought, 'he doesn't look very happy.'

'Richard is out, so you will eat with the servants in the kitchen,' said Aunt Rachel. 'I have told Cook to look after you.'

John and Patience were glad to spend the evening with Bess, the cook. They liked the warm, comfortable kitchen. It reminded them of the family parlour at home. In Aunt Rachel's kitchen, the cooking pans were made of copper, instead of iron, but the pewter mugs, the dresser and the big table were all very similar to the ones at home.

Bess was very friendly. She made them pancakes for supper and asked them about their family and the farm. 'Don't fret,' she said. 'You'll be home soon and will have lots to tell your folks about life in the big wide world! And let's see a smile on your face, too,' she said, looking at Jane, the new kitchen maid, 'your seven years will soon be over!'

Patience looked puzzled, so Jane explained.

'I come from England and I am an orphan. My parents were very poor when they died, and I had no one else to turn to. So I signed an agreement with your uncle to work for him for seven years if he would pay my fare over here. He is a kind master, but sometimes I miss my own country very much and feel like a prisoner. Bess here is a free woman; she could leave at any time she wanted. But I can't . . .' She bit her lip to stop herself from crying.

'Oh dear,' said Bess. 'Don't take on so! You're a good girl, and the master will give you some money when you've worked your seven years. And then you can buy some land and a nice young man will want to marry you, and you'll live happily ever after! Now, youngsters, it's time for bed! Take this warming pan, but mind you don't scorch the sheets.'

The Barn-raising

John and Patience climbed eagerly into the carriage
beside their uncle. They were going home! It was very
early in the morning and the Boston streets seemed
unusually quiet. Aunt Rachel and Cousin Priscilla
were still in bed. They had not returned from the ball
until two in the morning.

'They don't have to work for their living, like the
rest of us!' said Bess. 'When do I ever get a chance to
spend the morning in bed?'

Uncle Samuel's new carriage was too fine for
the rough country roads, so they left it at an inn and
hired an older one for the last part of their journey. As
they went down the steep hill that led to Saxmundham
they overtook Mr Mappin, the carpenter from
Blithborough. He was riding towards their village
with a huge cartload of timbers. He waved to the
children.

'So you've come home in good time, have you?' he
said. 'I didn't think you'd want to miss it!'

'Miss what?' shouted John and Patience together.

'Why, the barn-raising of course!' said Mr Mappin. 'I thought you knew all about it. Your father's re-building the old barn that burnt down last autumn. We set the frame up this morning and this timber here will go to make the rafters.'

John turned excitedly to his uncle. 'Have you ever been to a barn-raising, Uncle Samuel?' he asked. 'It's much more fun than any ball, I bet! The whole village will be there to help because no one's strong enough to build a barn by themselves. Last time, they let me climb on the roof. I could see for miles!'

'And you nearly fell and broke your neck,' said Patience. 'Stop showing off!'

Uncle Samuel laughed. 'It sounds like a lot of hard work to me! And rather dangerous!'

'Oh, barn-raisings are good fun, Uncle,' replied Patience. 'They're like a big party. We usually have lovely food, too, for a special treat. Last time we had smoked ham and gingerbread and cider. Mmm! You've been very kind to us, Uncle, and we're grateful, but it will be good to be home!'

27

Picture Glossary

The town of Boston owed its importance to its harbour, where large, ocean-going ships could shelter out of danger from the wild Atlantic storms. Dozens of jetties were built, stretching out into the waters of the harbour. The most important of these was Long Wharf, where up to 30 large ships could tie up at a time.

The town itself was built on an island which was joined to the mainland by a narrow 'neck' of land, like a causeway.

Strong gates guarded the entrance to the town. These were kept shut on Sundays.

Originally, all the buildings in Boston had been made of wood, cut from the vast forests of northern America. But most of the town was destroyed in the great fire which swept through the town in 1711. After this, the town governor declared that all new buildings should be made of brick, which would not catch fire so easily.

Above: Boston's old Town House, where the governing council sat. Merchants met in the market space underneath to make business deals. The building was burnt down in 1711.

Below: Map of the USA, showing Boston's position on the north-east coast.

Below: Map of Boston in 1728 showing its streets, the harbour and the numerous wharves.

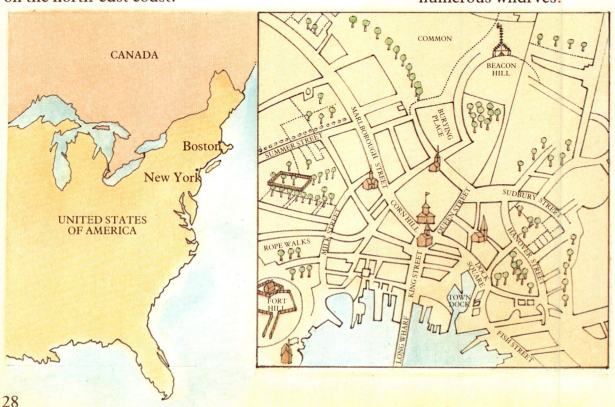

Left: Fashionable Boston

The Boston townspeople liked to copy European fashions, and eagerly waited for news of the latest trends from England and France. Wigs were especially popular. Here are some items that a fashionable man would have kept in his dressing room.

1 Bag wig.
2 Knotted wig.
3 Pipeclay wig curlers.
4 Wig stand.
5 Brass comb.
6 Two razors and case.
7 Silver and cockleshell snuff box.

Right: American silverware

8 Silver patch box, with 'trowel' to remove patches.
9 Tea caddy.
10 Sugar box.
11 Sugar cutters.
12 Tea pot.
13 Chocolate pot.
14 Invalid cup with spout for feeding.
15 Drinking bowl.

Right: Furniture

Wealthy people liked comfortable and beautiful objects in their homes. Specialist craftsmen made luxury goods in America, but the finest furniture was still imported from England.

16 Sewing table in walnut, with a slate top.
17 Chair made from maple.
18 American long-case clock.
19 Folding bed, made to save space.
20 Bed-wrench, used to tighten the bedropes which supported the soft feather mattress.

Finding Out More

Books to Read

G. Caselli **The Renaissance and the New World** (Macdonald 1985)

N. Grant **Everyday Life in the Eighteenth Century** (Macdonald 1983)

L. B. Wright **The Everyday Life in Colonial America** (Batsford 1965)

Places to Visit

Bath: American Museum, Claverton Manor
       Museum of Costume, The Assembly Rooms
London: National Maritime Museum
       Victoria and Albert Museum